Y 781.49 SCHAEFE
Schaefer, A. R. (Adam Richard),
Making a first recording /
33277002259583

CAMAS PUBLIC LIBRARY
CAMAS, WA

3 3277 00225 9583

D0792141

Rock Music Library

Making a First Recording

by A. R. Schaefer

Consultant: James Henke
Vice President of Exhibitions and Curatorial Affairs
Rock and Roll Hall of Fame and Museum
Cleveland, Ohio

Capstone press

Mankato, Minnesota

Camas Public Library

Capstone High-Interest Books are published by Capstone Press
151 Good Counsel Drive, P.O. Box 669, Mankato, Minnesota 56002
http://www.capstone-press.com

Copyright © 2004 by Capstone Press. All rights reserved.
No part of this publication may be reproduced in whole or in part, or stored in a retrieval
system, or transmitted in any form or by any means, electronic, mechanical,
photocopying, recording, or otherwise, without written permission of the publisher.
For information regarding permission, write to Capstone Press,
151 Good Counsel Drive, P.O. Box 669, Dept. R, Mankato, Minnesota 56002.
Printed in the United States of America

Library of Congress Cataloging-in-Publication Data
Schaefer, A. R. (Adam Richard), 1976–
    Making a first recording / by Adam Schaefer.
    p. cm.—(Rock music library)
    Summary: Describes the process of making a first recording, including the
responsibilities of the band members, recording options, and the roles of recording
studio professionals.
    Includes bibliographical references (p. 31) and index.
    ISBN 0-7368-2147-3 (hardcover)
    1. Sound recording industry—Vocational guidance—Juvenile literature.
2. Music trade—Vocational guidance—Juvenile literature. [1. Sound recording
industry. 2. Music trade.] I. Title. II. Series.
ML3790.S28 2004
781.49—dc21   2002155823

Editorial Credits

Carrie Braulick, editor; Jason Knudson; series designer; Jo Miller, photo researcher;
    Karen Risch, product planning editor

Photo Credits

Capstone Press/Gary Sundermeyer, cover, 5 (both), 6, 7, 9, 10 (both), 12, 13, 15, 16,
    19 (both), 20, 21, 23, 24, 26, 27, 28–29
Getty Images/Hulton Archive, 25

**Capstone Press thanks Two Fish Studios in Mankato, Minnesota, for their help
in preparing this book.**

1 2 3 4 5 6 08 07 06 05 04 03

Table of Contents

CHAPTER 1

The Recording Process

The band members enter the recording studio. High-tech equipment is lined up against the walls. Microphones hang from the ceiling. The band sets up and prepares for the session. They have been practicing for months to be ready for this day.

The drummer counts down the opening, and the band begins to play. The guitarist stops the song after only a few seconds. He makes a few adjustments on the amplifier, and the band starts again. Several hours later, the band has recorded 12 songs.

Learn about:

Producing a recording

Studio engineers

A first recording success

After months of practicing, the band members enter the recording studio prepared to make their first recording.

Recording studios have high-tech equipment such as mixing boards.

A studio engineer can guide band members through the recording process.

A few days later, the band meets with the studio engineer. The engineer adjusts the sound of the songs. The band walks out of the studio with a complete CD.

The band has 1,000 copies of the CD made. The band members give away copies to radio stations and fans. Soon, people begin buying the CD at local music stores and at the band's gigs.

Producing a Recording

Many bands have a goal to make a recording. With a recording, they can promote their music and sell CDs.

Bands work hard to make their recording successful. They practice to be sure they are prepared for the recording session. They make sure they produce the desired sound while recording. After the music is recorded onto a CD, the band works to make people aware of the album. They may sell copies of the CD.

Making a recording can help band members develop their musical talent.

CHAPTER 2

Preparing to Record

Making a recording can be stressful for a band. If it is the band's first recording, band members might feel pressure. The cost of making a recording can be very high. Band members want to produce a high-quality recording. Bands make decisions to help the recording session go smoothly.

Getting Ready

Band members need to make goals. Bands often want to create a CD to promote their music. Bands also could make a single tape or CD to send to local radio stations.

Learn about:

Making a playlist

Home studios

Professional studios

Band members can help the studio engineer prepare for a recording.

Some bands make a demo tape or CD to send to a record company.

After band members decide on a goal, they choose a lineup of songs. Most groups decide on a playlist that shows all of their talents. Bands often include both fast songs and slow songs to create variety on the recording.

Setting up equipment properly is an important part of producing a recording.

Guitarists should take time to warm up before a recording session.

Bands practice the songs on their playlist before the recording session. If a band member does not know the music or forgets words, the band will waste time in the recording studio.

Types of Studios

Bands can record music in a home studio or at a professional studio. Band members who set up a home studio must make sure they have proper recording equipment. Basic equipment includes speakers, microphones, and a recorder. Bands also need a mixer to adjust the sound of a recording.

Most bands record their music in professional studios. These studios have recording equipment available. They also have staff members who can help guide bands through the recording process.

"The advantage of having a home studio is being able to lock the door and not let anyone in! Having a studio at home is definitely a safety zone."

—Dave Grohl, lead singer of the Foo Fighters

Professional Studios

Most professional studios include a producer and a sound engineer. The producer is in charge of the entire recording project. The studio engineer controls the sound of the recording.

Most studios are divided into two rooms. The band members often play in a soundproof room to prevent outside sounds from affecting the recording. The producer and the sound engineer direct the session from the control room.

Musicians wear headphones so they can hear themselves play.

High-quality microphones in recording studios easily pick up sound.

Band members do research to find a studio that will fit their needs. Band members also meet the studio staff. This meeting helps them learn about the skills and knowledge of the producer and studio engineer. The band members make sure they are comfortable in the studio. The studio should be large enough for the band's equipment.

CHAPTER 3

Laying the Tracks

After band members find a studio, they reserve a block of studio time. As the recording day nears, the band makes final preparations. Band members continue to practice the playlist. They get enough rest before the session. Singers rest their voices.

On recording day, band members pack backup equipment in case an instrument breaks during the session. Bands may bring extra guitar strings, drumsticks, guitar picks, and even extra instruments to a recording session.

Learn about:

Setting up equipment

Multi-track recordings

Direct-to-two-track recordings

Guitarists should listen carefully to the sound of their guitar before recording.

At the Studio

After the band arrives at the studio, the members meet the studio engineer and set up the equipment. Band members set up the equipment in a way that allows them to see each other. This arrangement allows the band members to easily communicate with one another.

After the equipment is set up, the band members take a few minutes to tune their instruments and warm up. They make any necessary adjustments to the equipment. The audio levels may need to be adjusted. Proper audio levels provide a good balance between instruments and singers.

Preparation before a recording session takes time, but it is worth it. A prepared band will not need to play songs several times to make them sound right. Bands usually rent studio time by the hour, so preparation can help bands save money.

The time band members spend preparing will be worth it after they start to record.

Copyright Law

Copyright law is designed to protect a musician's work. The law tells people what they are allowed to do with someone else's music.

To play other musicians' songs for large audiences, bands must receive permission first. Some of these bands are known as "cover bands." Cover bands almost always play songs that other bands have recorded. The American Society of Composers, Authors, and Publishers (ASCAP) gives bands permission to perform many songs produced in the United States. BMI and SESAC are other performing rights organizations.

Bands also must receive permission to record another musician's work. The Harry Fox Agency is the main organization that provides these licenses to musicians in the United States.

Recording

Most bands produce multi-track recordings through a process called overdubbing. In these recording sessions, the sound engineer first records each instrument separately. The sound engineer then plays the music back and records any vocals on the song. When band members concentrate on playing their instruments, they usually produce a better recording. Recording the instruments first also makes it easier for the sound engineer to mix the recording one instrument at a time.

Some bands use the direct-to-two-track recording method. This recording method uses one recorder and one or two microphones. The instruments and voices are recorded at the same time. The direct-to-two-track method works well when bands are recording songs without electric instruments.

During the multi-track recording method, each instrument is recorded onto a separate track.

Vocals can be recorded in separate soundproof rooms.

Using Time Wisely

A band needs to use its recording time wisely. Some beginning bands get nervous in the studio. Band members may worry about the quality of the recording or about the money the studio time costs. They may start to rush through the recording. If band members rush, the quality of the recording can suffer. A bad recording will not sell or help a band schedule gigs.

Band members should try to prevent one another from getting too nervous. They can tell jokes or take short breaks to relax.

A professional recording studio is equipped with amplifiers and microphones.

"It takes a while for five people to make the same noise—to get together and head in the same direction."

—Rob Thomas, lead singer of Matchbox Twenty

Good communication during a recording session can help band members produce a high-quality recording.

CHAPTER 4

After the Session

Making a recording is only part of the process. A multi-track recording still needs to be mixed. After the recording is finished, copies can be made. The band can give away or sell the copies to fans.

Mixing

To mix a recording, a sound engineer adjusts the levels to get the sound the band wants. For a multi-track recording, an engineer usually starts mixing the drums. The engineer can take each drum and make it louder or softer on the recording. An engineer can make adjustments to make the beats and notes sound different.

Learn about:

Mixing

Promotion and distribution

Expectations

Studio engineers mix a recording to make final adjustments.

After mixing the drums, the engineer mixes the other instruments and the voices. When all the songs are done, they are put in order and recorded onto a tape or CD called the master copy.

Promotion and Distribution

Most bands promote and distribute their recording on their own. Few bands who send their demo tape or CD to a record company receive a contract. Competition for record company contracts is high.

Bands can promote a recording in various ways. Band members may ask local radio stations to mention their CD on the air. Some bands play a free concert to celebrate the release of their CD. They also can book gigs to make more people aware of their band.

Distributing an album to the public is important for bands. Bands can ask local record stores to sell their CD. They may give copies away or sell them to fans at gigs. Bands also can sell their CD on the Internet.

An interview on a local radio station can be a good way to promote a new CD.

Creed

In 1995, Scott Stapp, Mark Tremonti, Brian Marshall, and Scott Phillips formed Creed in Tallahassee, Florida. Marshall later left the group. Creed became one of the most popular rock bands of the late 1990s and early 2000s. In 1997, the band released its first CD, *My Own Prison*. It became the first debut album in history to have four number one singles on the rock radio airplay charts. The CD has sold more than 6 million copies. Creed's second CD, *Human Clay*, went diamond, selling more than 10 million copies. In 1998, 1999, and 2000, the group won Billboard's Rock Artist of the Year award. One of their songs, "With Arms Wide Open," won a Grammy Award in 2001.

Expectations

Some bands make a profit by selling their CD to local fans. Other bands sell few CDs and do not even meet the cost of making the recording. Months often go by before fans begin buying an album.

Band members may ask local music store owners to sell their CD.

Some music stores have separate racks where local CDs are displayed.

Sometimes, bands do not meet the goals they try to accomplish by producing a recording. Their CD may not sell as well as they had planned. Their recording may be turned down by a radio station. But these bands should still be proud of their achievement. Making a first recording is a learning experience that helps band members become better musicians.

Designing a CD Cover

After producing a CD, you can design a cover for it. The cover should represent your band and its music. The following guidelines can help you create a cover that will help sell the CD.

1 The cover should attract attention. The name of the band on the front cover should be clear and easy to read.

THE ROCKS

2 The inside of the cover should give more information about the band or the CD. You may want to include pictures of the band or song lyrics.

THE ROCKS

Marsh

Sweet Mosquito

Saturday I called but you're never home
Still my friends they say that it'll be okay
But what do they know

Then on Sunday you call to apologize
Say you were busy and couldn't see me
What am I doing next Fri

So the week comes and goes sitting by the phone,
But it doesn't matter at all cuz you never call
Until you're feeling alone

Then Friday comes and I fall for it again
The Saturday blow off and Sunday call up
To ask if we're still friends

Recorded at:
Two Fish Studios
All songs written by:
The Rocks

Johnny, vocals
Matt, bass
Shanna, guitar
Frank-O, drums

3 *The back cover should list the song titles. Some bands also list the length of each song.*

THE **ROCKS**

1. sweet mosquito (3:21)
2. angry green (2:55)
3. lounge lizard (2:45)
4. the apes are loose (4:10)
5. spaghetti overload (3:21)
6. raining hot dogs (8:54)

4 *The spine should list the CD and band name.*

THE **ROCKS**   6 SONG DEMO

5 *The design should be uniform. For example, the same colors or the same graphic can be used throughout the cover design.*

THE **ROCKS**

THE **ROCKS**

THE **ROCKS**

1. sweet mosquito (3:21)
2. angry green (2:55)
3. lounge lizard (2:45)
4. the apes are loose (4:10)
5. spaghetti overload (3:21)
6. raining hot dogs (8:54)

Glossary

contract (KON-trakt)—a legal agreement between people stating the terms by which one will work for the other

distribute (diss-TRIB-yoot)—to deliver CDs to record stores and other places

engineer (en-juh-NIHR)—someone who is trained to work on mixing boards and other equipment in recording studios

gig (GIG)—a live performance in front of an audience

master copy (MAS-tur KOP-ee)—the final recording that a band produces before more copies are made

mixer (MIKS-ur)—an electronic device that adjusts sounds on a track

overdub (oh-vur-DUB)—to record sounds onto an existing track

playlist (PLAY-list)—a list of songs to be played or recorded

promote (pruh-MOTE)—to make the public aware of a band's CD

track (TRAK)—recorded sound laid along the length of a magnetic tape

To Learn More

Belleville, Nyree. *Booking, Promoting, and Marketing Your Music.* Ann Arbor, Mich.: MixBooks, 2000.

Morgan, Sally, and Pauline Lalor. *Music.* Behind Media. Chicago: Heinemann Library, 2001.

Rosenthal, Michèle. *Rock Rules!: The Ultimate Rock Band Book.* New York: Scholastic, 2000.

Useful Addresses

Harry Fox Agency, Inc.
711 Third Avenue
New York, NY 10017

Recording Industry Association of America
1330 Connecticut Avenue NW
Suite 300
Washington, DC 20036

Rock and Roll Hall of Fame and Museum
One Key Plaza
Cleveland, OH 44114

Rolling Stone Magazine
1290 Avenue of the Americas
New York, NY 10104-0298

Internet Sites

Do you want to find out more about rock bands?
Let FactHound, our fact-finding hound dog, do the research for you.

Here's how:

1) Visit *http://www.facthound.com*
2) Type in the **Book ID** number: **0736821473**
3) Click on **FETCH IT**.

FactHound will fetch Internet sites picked by our editors just for you!

Index